THE STORYTIME SURPRISE

Vini Nair

For my son, whose courage and belief in me never waver, thank you for cheering me on. You remind me to be brave, to try again and to believe in myself. Your creativity, your humour and your joyful spirit inspire me every day. A little piece of your laughter and love is tucked into every page of this story.

And to my students, whose imaginations have no limits, thank you for your curious questions, your wonderful ideas and the colourful way you see the world.

This story holds a tiny piece of all your courage, creativity, giggles and joy.

The teacher asked the children,
"Which book would you like to read today?"
Noah and Veda pointed at 2 different books,
"Not that one! We read it yesterday!" screamed Zara
"I want the dinosaur book!" roared Noah.

"Nooo, not dinosaurs again!" groaned Meera.

"This one!" cheered Emily, holding up a red book.

"I didn't like that one," muttered Christopher.

"I like the book with the funny bear," yelped Oliver.

"The bear is silly," giggled Rayan.

This one!
That one!
That one!

The classroom buzzed with little roars, yelps, giggles, and mutters.
"Let's remember our 5 Ls," The teacher reminded gently.
"Hands in the air, hands on your shoulders, hands in your lap.
Listening ears, lips locked, and cross your legs," she chimed.
Little feet shuffled, little hands held tight,
Slowly, the room became quiet and still.

"How about we make our own story?" asked the teacher.

"Yayyy! Me, me!" cheered Oliver

"Can we have a dragon?" begged Christopher.

"Not a dragon again", teased Emily.

"Maybe a friendly one", blushed Christopher.

"And a fairy!" added Sofia.

"And a rocket ship!" shouted Rohan.

"And a rainbow!" whispered Tanvi.

"And space!" yelled Kai.

"All right!" the teacher smiled and said, "Let's make a story together."

"Once there was a dinosaur!" started Noah.

"And a baby!" said Anaya.

"The baby was crying," added Leo sadly.

"Oh no! Why was the baby crying?" asked the teacher.

"The mum didn't know," shrugged Oliver.

"Mum brought some fruit,"
said Veda.
But the baby said,
"No!"

No!

Mum brought yoghurt," said
Aarav.
But the baby said,
"No!"

No!

"Mum brought some lollies!" shouted
Kai.
But the baby said,
"No!"

No!

" Oh dear! Then what happened?" asked the teacher.
"Mum looked in the fridge," whispered Tanvi.
"But there was no milk!"

"So Mum went outside to milk the cow," murmured Rohan with a cheeky smile.

swish
swish

"And the baby followed her," added Sofia.

"And the dinosaur followed too!" laughed Noah.

?
waaa!

"Then a calf came over," said Christopher.

?
Pat Pat Pat

"SLURP! The calf licked the baby!" chirped
Arjun.
"The baby paused! and then started laughing!"
giggled Zara.

Slurp!

"Then the baby followed the calf," cheered Leo.

"The dinosaur followed too!" cackled Noah

"SLURP! The calf licked the baby again!"
said Zara with a chuckle.
"The baby giggled, rolling on the floor!" laughed Rayan.
"They all played together!" the children cheered.

"Mum offered some milk!" exclaimed Emily with

a cheeky laugh.

But the baby said, "No!"

"The baby just wanted to play with the calf!"

The children said together.

"And the dinosaur!" roared Noah.

No!

The teacher's face lit up
with a warm smile and she said,
"What a wonderful thought! Sometimes all
we really need is a happy friend to play with."

THE END

ABOUT THE AUTHOR

Vini Nair is a passionate teacher who believes in the magic of imagination, curiosity, and joyful learning. She believes that everyone is a storyteller. Articulating thoughts and verbalising feelings are not only a challenge for young ones but for grown-ups too. She does not look for following trends, patterns, or sticking strictly to rules while expressing imagination. Instead, she is passionate about inspiring children to express themselves beyond set patterns, letting their ideas and creativity flow naturally. The artists who have created outside the patterns are often the ones remembered beyond their time. Inspired daily by the children she teaches and encouraged by her creative, fun-loving son, Vineeta loves creating stories that spark wonder, laughter, and the joy of discovering oneself.

Vini Nair

www.ingramcontent.com/pod-product-compliance
Lightning Source LLC
Chambersburg PA
CBHW080506030726
47592CB00011B/3271